MW01147218

THE GHOSTLY TALES OF SAN ANTONIO

Get into the
spirit of reading!

Jay Whistler

Published by Arcadia Children's Books
A Division of Arcadia Publishing
Charleston, SC
www.arcadiapublishing.com

Copyright © 2021 by Arcadia Children's Books
All rights reserved

Spooky America is a trademark of Arcadia Publishing, Inc.

First published 2021

Manufactured in the United States

ISBN 978-1-4671-9812-7

Library of Congress Control Number: 2021938349

Notice: The information in this book is true and complete to the best of our knowledge. It is offered without guarantee on the part of the author or Arcadia Publishing. The author and Arcadia Publishing disclaim all liability in connection with the use of this book.

All rights reserved. No part of this book may be reproduced or transmitted in any form whatsoever without prior written permission from the publisher except in the case of brief quotations embodied in critical articles and reviews.

Images courtesy of Shutterstock.com; p. 2 xradiophotog/Shutterstock.com; p. 28 Salvador Aznar/Shutterstock.com; p. 56 Dietmar Rauscher/Shutterstock.com; p. 68 Moab Republic/Shutterstock.com

Adapted from *Haunted History of Old San Antonio* by Lauren M. Swartz and James A. Swartz

arcadia
CHILDREN'S BOOKS

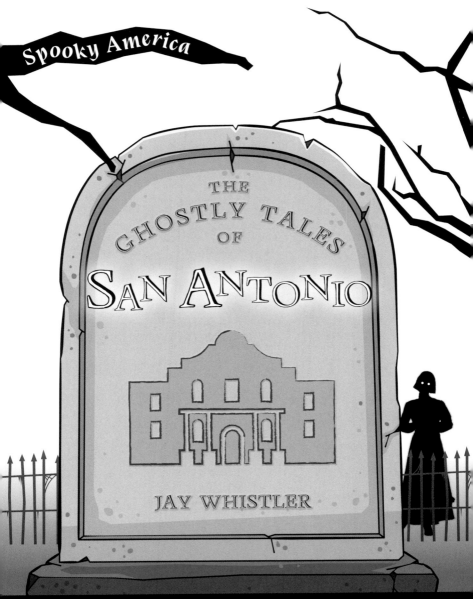

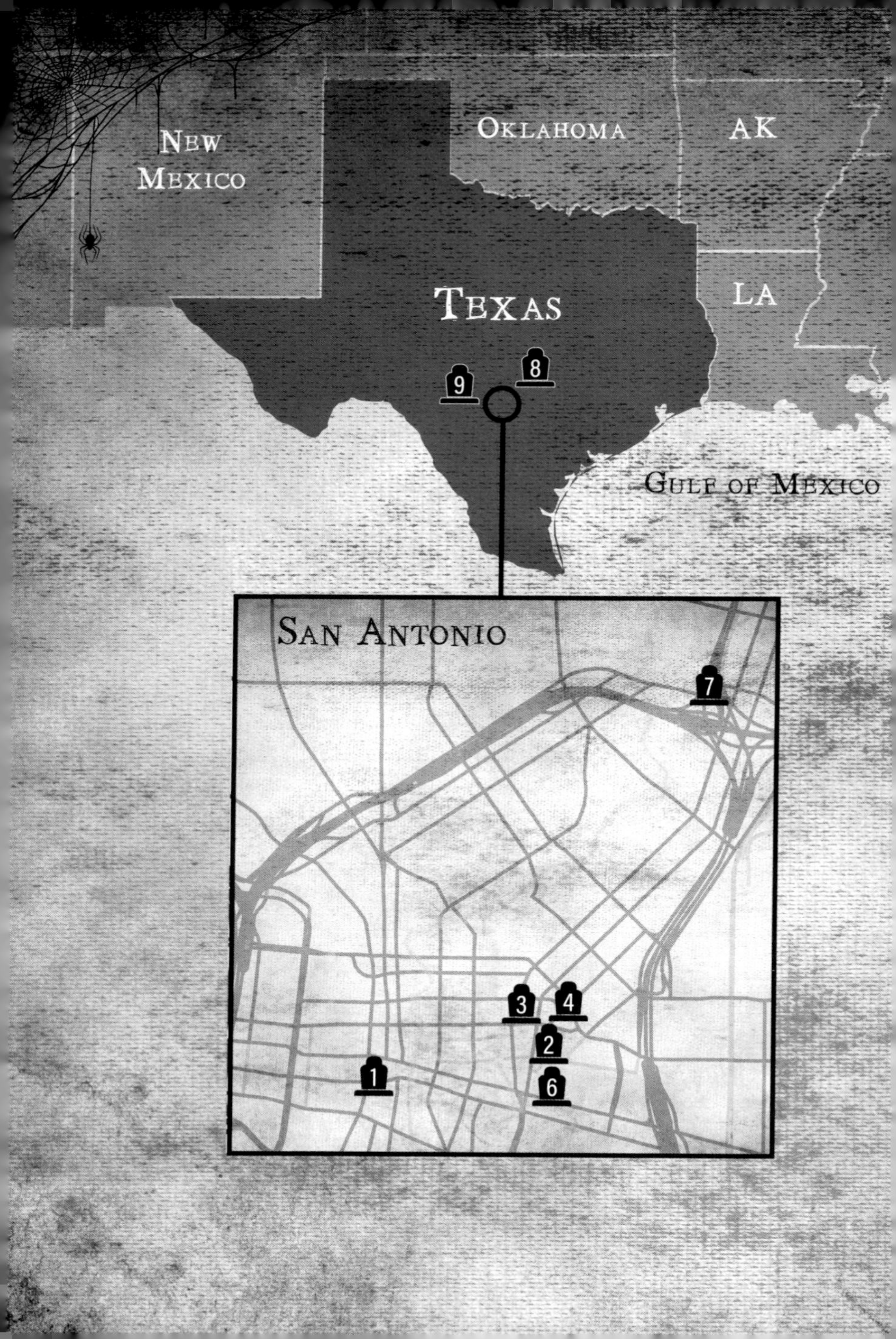

New Mexico
Oklahoma
AK
Texas
LA
Gulf of Mexico
San Antonio
1
2
3
4
6
7
8
9

Table of Contents & Map Key

North Star Mall Boots

Introduction

There's no place like San Antonio, Texas. The Alamo City. Home of the River Walk, Tower of the Americas, and the world's largest pair of cowboy boots.

San Antonio was settled on May 1, 1718, when a Spanish expedition from Mexico established the Mission San Antonio de Valero, one of a series of five missions built in the area by Catholic missionaries from Spain and

Mexico. The missions served two purposes: first, as lodging for missionaries working in Texas, and second, as centers for missionaries to carry out their goal to convert indigenous populations to Christianity and Catholicism.

Although the official name is Mission San Antonio de Valero, after the Portuguese Saint Anthony of Padua, the mission was eventually nicknamed the Alamo, which is Spanish for "cottonwood," a tree popular with settlers and travelers because it signaled water nearby or

within easy digging distance for wells. In those days, cottonwood trees thrived throughout San Antonio, with thick stands along the river.

Today, the mission system in San Antonio is part of the National Park System and is a designated UNESCO World Heritage site, recognized and protected so future generations can learn about and enjoy all the missions.

Tourists come from all over the world to visit the Alamo and other missions. While they are in town, they might cheer on the brave and daring riders at the rodeo or visit the Tower of the Americas, a 750-foot observation tower built for the 1968 World's Fair and standing 145 feet taller than Seattle's Space Needle! Locals and visitors alike can't get enough of the fast-paced action at the AT&T Center, home of the five-time NBA champion San Antonio Spurs, one of the most successful franchises in all of American sports. People love to take selfies next to a pair of forty-foot-tall cowboy boots, officially recognized by the *Guinness Book of World Records* as the largest in the world in 2016, a full thirty-seven years after they were built by Bob "Daddy-O" Wade as an

outdoor sculpture in Washington, DC. Only six months after their installation in DC, the boots arrived in San Antonio, and they have graced the entrance to the North Star Mall ever since.

Travelers also wander the River Walk, a series of trails along the San Antonio River, where visitors can shop, grab a bite to eat, or float down the river in guided tour boats that give an impressive overview of Texas history, from its early days as a Spanish settlement, its time as a Mexican territory, its importance in the battle of the Alamo, and its years as its own country right up to modern times.

You may be wondering what history has to do with ghost stories and haunted buildings. Let's take a walk through the haunted history of San Antonio to find out.

San Fernando Cathedral

CHAPTER 1

San Fernando Cathedral and Main Plaza

Twenty-three years after San Antonio was settled by the first Mexican missionaries, Spanish settlers from the Canary Islands arrived in 1731 with plans to build a community in honor of Spain's King Ferdinand III, who sent the islanders to claim the territory. That community included the San Fernando Cathedral.

Soon after the settlers began building the cathedral, they fought with the native indigenous Lipan Apache people for control of the area. In 1749, a truce was arranged between the settlers and the Apache. As part of a ceremony to celebrate the truce, the Apache dug a giant hole in the main plaza in front of the cathedral. Inside, they lay down their hatchets, arrows, and war clubs to symbolize their commitment to peace. This was a common practice in those days, and it is the origin of the phrase "bury the hatchet," which means to agree to peacefully settle differences.

After the truce with the Lipan Apache was declared, the settlers finished the cathedral in 1755, and it went on to become central to the daily life of the townsfolk. A plaza rose up in front of the cathedral, filled with market stalls where San

Antonians could buy meat or dairy products from the local cattle rancher, eggs from the local poultry farmer, bolts of fabric from the local weaver, and more. There was also a community well for fresh water. In addition to the temporary market stalls, hotels, saloons, and other businesses set up more permanent buildings.

Now considered the oldest standing structure in all of Texas, San Fernando Cathedral became the geographic center of San Antonio, and all distances in the city were physically measured from the cross erected on the center of the cathedral's dome. Today, there is a brass marker in the floor beneath the dome declaring that spot as the geographical center of San Antonio.

For many years, San Fernando Cathedral and San Antonio remained part of Mexico, even serving as the capital of the Mexican province of Tejas, the Spanish spelling of a Native American Caddo word roughly translating to "friend" or "ally." The province eventually became known as Texas.

Almost a hundred years after the Canary Islanders arrived, James Bowie settled in San Antonio in 1830 as a colonel in the Texas Rangers, a volunteer group that protected the residents of the area. He married in the San Fernando Cathedral in 1831. In 1833, Bowie sent his wife and young children out of San Antonio, because he feared an epidemic of cholera was on its way to the city. Sadly, the epidemic skipped the city and instead landed where his wife and children were staying. The entire family contracted the disease and perished. Bowie was inconsolable and never got over the loss of his family. Bowie's remains are said to be in a white sarcophagus near the front entrance of the cathedral.

Visitors to the cathedral claim to have been followed by an apparition that appears quickly then disappears just as fast. No one knows for sure if it is the ghost of James Bowie, but it would be understandable if it were. Who could blame him if this is where his spirit feels the most connected to his family?

It's impossible to think of San Antonio and not be reminded of the Alamo. The former mission stands half a mile from the cathedral and became a military fort during the Texas Revolution. For over three hundred years, from the time the Europeans first explored the area now known as Texas in 1519 until 1848, five different countries claimed all or part of the state as their own. France, Spain, Mexico, and the United States fought for control. And for a brief time, the Republic of Texas was its own country.

In 1835, Mexico's president, General Antonio López de Santa Anna, dissolved Mexico's constitution, prompting Texas's fight for independence and the start of the Texas Revolution. General Santa Anna himself led the Mexican Army into San Antonio to regain control of the region. He set up camp in the shadow of the San Fernando Cathedral, where he and his soldiers were out of range of the Alamo's weapons. Meanwhile, a hundred Texian soldiers stood by to protect the Alamo from invasion.

On February 23, Santa Anna and his soldiers attacked the Alamo, trapping the Texian soldiers inside. The soldiers were unprepared and had very little food, water, or gunpowder. James Bowie and his co commander, William Travis, sent urgent messages to other Texian Army regiments begging for reinforcements to help push back the Mexican Army. One rescue party tried to reach the Alamo but only managed to travel a couple miles from its own fort when news that a Mexican Army regiment was on its way to intercept the party forced the mission to be abandoned.

However, a small group of volunteers eventually reached the Alamo, and under cover of darkness, they made it inside to

provide supplies and extra firepower, helping the Texians hold off Mexican forces a few more days. Commander Bowie, still grieving over the loss of his family but determined to keep the fort from enemy hands, lost his battle with yellow fever within the Alamo compound shortly after the fort received the extra supplies.

While all this was going on, a group of politicians met in a distant town to formally adopt the Texas Declaration of Independence. Soldiers at the besieged fort had no idea they were fighting for the new country of the Republic of Texas. Sadly, they would never know, because on March 6, General Santa Anna's troops engaged in one final battle, leaving nearly all one hundred Texian soldiers dead.

Santa Anna had promised "no quarter" to the Texian soldiers, meaning he would not take them as prisoners even if they surrendered. After his victory at the Alamo, he lived up to his word and refused even the most basic burial for the Texians who had given their lives. Instead, their remains were thrown into bonfires. After the fires were out and Santa Anna and his soldiers left the area, residents near the bonfires are said to have retrieved some of the bones and asked the monks to bury them in the cathedral.

Paranormal experts claim that traumatic events leave negative psychic energy in a space. Over the years, many tourists at the San Fernando Cathedral have reported red orbs appearing in photos or visible to the naked eye. Maybe these orbs are the specters of wounded Mexican soldiers who made it back to their camp near the cathedral before perishing. They could be

the ghostly echo of the flames set by General Santa Anna. Or they might be symbolic of the bloodshed from the battle. Whatever they represent, the orbs are manifestations of the former violence on the steps of the cathedral.

But the San Fernando Cathedral did not always have such a negative history. Hundreds of years ago, it was common practice for the clergy, wealthy church members, or other dignitaries to be buried within the church itself, for a fee. This helped finance construction. San Fernando Cathedral was no different, and donors' earthly remains are still inside the cathedral to this day. Some people believe it is these wealthy patrons whose ghostly images wander the pews and appear to the cathedral's visitors. For example, it could be the spirit of a wealthy female donor buried in the walls who appeared in a photo taken by a member of a San Antonio ghost tour. She seemed to float above the entire group in her long dress. Or it could be one of the clergy buried there who wander around the sanctuary wearing the traditional hood of Catholic monks. What stories do these old bones know?

But the eeriest appearance may be the outline of a skull in the rock wall near the rear of the cathedral. The image shows deep eye sockets, a long nose, and a grim mouth, and some paranormal investigators think it might be Anthony Dominic Pellicer, the first bishop of San Fernando Cathedral. Whether it is the bishop or a messenger from the past, we may never know what message the skull is trying to tell us.

CHAPTER 2

Hotel Gibbs

In San Antonio's Main Plaza sit three hotels, all of which are rumored to be haunted. Hotel Gibbs, built on what used to be the northwest corner of the Alamo, began life as the first skyscraper in San Antonio and is the only hotel on the plaza standing directly on the former battlefield, which may be one of the reasons it is considered haunted. Several important events, and three prominent San Antonians, have left their mark on the hotel.

The first prominent San Antonian to leave his mark is William Travis, the co commander, along with James Bowie, of the battle of the Alamo. Before becoming a commander, Travis came from Alabama to Texas and soon joined the Texian Army, eventually becoming a lieutenant colonel. He was ordered to take his unit to provide reinforcements at the Alamo, where he joined commander James Bowie's unit, and the two became co-commanders for the duration of the battle.

On March 6, 1836, Mexican soldiers stormed the Alamo in what became the bloodiest and final day of the thirteen-day siege. Texian soldiers, weak from lack of food and almost out of ammunition, stood no chance of fighting back. Travis knew the odds of survival were slim. He even wrote a letter during the siege in which he admitted he was unlikely to see the end of the battle. He signed the letter, "Victory or Death!"

When General Santa Anna stormed the fort, Travis was one of the first on the battlefield, shouting encouragement to his troops. A bullet struck him early in the fight as the Mexican Army breached the walls. But he continued to fight with his sword, holding off attackers even as he slowly bled to death. The spot on which Travis finally fell is where the front desk of the Hotel Gibbs now stands.

Guests of the hotel claim to hear Travis shouting "Come on, boys!" and other encouragement to his men, as if he still fights General Santa Anna and the Mexican Army.

Another prominent citizen to have an impact on Hotel Gibbs was Samuel Maverick. Nearly all the Texians quartered at the former mission were killed in battle. Most of those who survived were executed rather than taken prisoner. One of the few survivors was a man named Samuel Maverick, who had left the fort just a few days before it fell. He managed to make the trip to the Convention of 1836 in time to sign the Texas Declaration of Independence on March 2, just four days before the fort was stormed for the final time. Several years later, in 1839, he was elected mayor of San Antonio.

Maverick became a cattle rancher and a land baron, owning over 66,000 acres, or more than 103 square miles. That's roughly the size of Amarillo! Maverick was also known for failing to brand his cattle, and soon any unbranded cattle found roaming the range were known as "mavericks." The term also became synonymous with someone who possessed a stubborn, independent streak.

In 1852, Maverick began construction of a home on the northwest corner of the Alamo mission grounds, because as he said, "I have a desire to reside in this particular spot. A foolish prejudice, no doubt, as I was almost a solitary escape from the Alamo massacre."

While excavating the new construction, crews found thirteen of the twenty-one original cannons used in the Battle of the Alamo. The family donated all of them to the mission, where they are still on display.

After his home was transformed into an office building and then a hotel, Maverick appears to wander the halls of the Hotel Gibbs in search of his fallen comrades, and guests frequently report hearing cannon fire, screams, and other sounds of the bloody battle. Maybe it is Maverick himself whose footsteps echo in the basement of the hotel, a reminder of when he excavated the cannons. Some hotel guests have seen what

appear to be Texian soldiers charging against their attackers, forever defending the fort in vain.

In 1909, Colonel Charles C. Gibbs, an executive with Southern Pacific Railroad, began construction of the Gibbs Building. Two more cannons were unearthed in the basement of the former Maverick homestead. One of the cannons was given to the Briscoe Western Art Museum, a few blocks south of the hotel. The other was given to the Alamo mission.

Shortly thereafter, a postal worker claimed to see two men pushing a cannon near the construction site of the hotel in the early dawn. He assumed it was being moved to prepare for a battle reenactment. But no reenactment was scheduled to take place, and no one can explain how the cannon was moved that day from its location at the mission to the plaza.

When the Gibbs office building opened in the early twentieth century, visitors enjoyed the ultra modern convenience of its elegant elevators, and they were greeted by operators in blue uniforms with white gloves right up until 2006.

Despite no longer being in use, these elevators tend to confuse some guests, who are convinced they see a woman dressed in 1940s attire exiting the elevator while the elevator operator in his blue suit stands at attention in the background.

If you visit the Hotel Gibbs, maybe you will see Samuel Maverick searching for other Alamo survivors. Maybe you'll see one of the original elevator operators open elevator doors for a passenger, even when those doors are now permanently sealed. Or you might be lucky enough to watch a ghostly cannon roll across the plaza!

The Emily Morgan Hotel

CHAPTER 3

The Emily Morgan Hotel

About one hundred feet north of the Alamo stands a majestic Gothic structure constructed in 1924 as the most advanced medical arts building west of the Mississippi River. Sixty years later, the building was turned into the luxury Emily Morgan Hotel. In 2015, *USA Today* named the Emily Morgan Hotel the third-most haunted hotel in the world, making it the most haunted hotel in Texas.

It may seem strange for a former medical building to be renamed after an indentured person from the mid-1800s. But local lore says Emily Morgan played a pivotal role in the fight for Texas independence, and her legend lives on with a hotel named in her honor.

Emily West was born in 1815 in New Haven, Connecticut, as a free woman of mixed race. When she was twenty, she was indentured for one year to James Morgan as a housekeeper for the New Washington Hotel in Morgan's Point, Texas, a small town on the Gulf of Mexico. Although technically an employee, West took on the last name of her employer—a common practice in those days—and became Emily Morgan. Several months later, she and other employees were kidnapped by Mexican cavalry, and Morgan wound up a prisoner of General Santa Anna.

In April 1836, General Santa Anna, still feeling confident after a successful battle at the Alamo a month earlier, prepared to battle the Texian Army, led by General Sam Houston, who would later become the first president of the new Republic of Texas. Against advice from some of his officers, General Santa Anna made camp near the San Jacinto River. The spot was particularly vulnerable, according to historians, due to the woods on one side and marshy terrain on the other.

On April 21, at 4:30 p.m., Texian soldiers fired two cannons into the Mexican camp, beginning the Battle of San Jacinto. Immediately, the Texians stormed toward the enemy, shouting their now-famous cry of "Remember the Alamo!" In only fifteen minutes, the battle was over, and Texas had won. Santa Anna was captured the next day and, in exchange for his life, helped negotiate Mexico's official recognition of Texas as an independent country.

Historians say Santa Anna lost the battle because he made a poor decision about where to camp. Legend says he was not prepared when the battle began but was instead in his tent. Emily Morgan knew how important it was to keep Santa Anna from overseeing the battle, and the stories say she purposely distracted the general. Without his direction and encouragement, many Mexican soldiers retreated, leaving the remaining troops vulnerable to Texas's assault.

Emily Morgan's contribution to the Battle of San Jacinto, which ended the Texas Revolution, was later immortalized in the famous song "The Yellow Rose of Texas." Whether Morgan truly managed

to keep General Santa Anna from fulfilling his duties remains unclear. Historians say there is little evidence in the written record Morgan was present for the battle. However, a passage in the diary of William Bollaert, a British traveler, attributes the battle's success to "the influence of a . . . girl belonging to Colonel Morgan." Bollaert claimed he received this information directly from Sam Houston himself.

Whether Emily Morgan can be credited with single-handedly ending the Texas Revolution may never be known. What is known is she survived the battle, served the remainder of her indenture to Colonel Morgan, and left Texas for New York in 1837.

When the Medical Arts Building opened in 1924, one of the most striking features of the Gothic structure was the gargoyles, which experts say all depict different maladies, such as the figure with a hooked nose and scowling face who seems to be in pain. There are also figures clutching their stomachs or heads, and one face has what looks like a modern Band-Aid on its nose!

For fifty-two years, the building housed medical offices and a hospital. In 1976, it was converted to office space. Only eight years later, it became the Emily Morgan Hotel. Hotel staff say guests began having strange experiences almost immediately after the hotel opened. Floors seven, nine, and fourteen appear to be the most haunted, which makes sense when you consider they used to house the psychiatric wing, the surgery, and the morgue. Today, modern surgical techniques and improved mental health treatment mean patients and their families throughout San Antonio, and the country, receive the best care possible. In the first half of the twentieth century, however, patients with mental health challenges were often called "crazy" or "insane" and put in hospitals where, instead of receiving treatment, they might endure electroshock therapy or even receive lobotomies, a form of brain surgery thought to eliminate certain behaviors. More often, though, lobotomies made patients worse, left them with traumatic brain injuries, or resulted in their deaths.

Guests on the seventh, ninth, and fourteenth floors have seen and heard a variety of strange things such as lights flashing, bathroom faucets turning on and off by themselves, or doors opening and closing on their own. In hallways, some people have felt someone or something brush against them as they walk. Cold spots seem to linger as if a specter had recently passed through the area.

Some hotel guests have opened the door to their hotel

rooms and seen what looked like surgeons operating on a patient. For those who have witnessed this macabre scene, closing the door and slowly reopening it seems to clear the ghostly vision.

On the seventh floor, guests have heard a woman screaming as she runs down the hall. Her voice drifts to other floors but is most active and loudest here. When staff have investigated the source, they have found no explanation for the repeated occurrences. Perhaps she is someone from the surgery ward mourning the loss of a loved one, or a patient screaming in pain. Whoever she is, she visits the seventh floor again and again and again.

Staff have reported elevators traveling up and down with no passengers. Every so often, the front desk receives a phone call with no one on the other end. When the calls have been traced, they are coming from the empty elevators!

These elevators also tend to sneak hotel guests down to the basement, where the crematorium was once housed. They get quite a shock when the doors open and they discover disembodied voices, echoing

footsteps, or orbs of light floating in the air. Some people have even reported the smell of the crematorium as if it were still active.

All of these experiences are like watching the same show on TV over and over again. The action never changes. But every so often, a guest will interact with a phantom. One night, a young girl staying at the hotel with her family was awakened by a presence standing over her. She could see a tall, dark outline of a figure with no face. The figure pointed to the door, and the girl felt as if it were asking her to follow it out of the room. Frightened, she pulled the covers over her head and waited. Finally, she felt the presence disappear, and when she uncovered her face, it was gone. It's a good thing the girl stayed in bed, because no one knows where the figure wanted to take her.

Then there is the experience a mother and daughter shared one night as they got ready for bed. The mother climbed into bed and waited for her daughter to finish in the bathroom. When the mother felt the bed move and the covers rustle, she said, "You forgot to turn out the light." From the bathroom, her daughter answered, "I'm not done yet." The mother turned to find the blankets raised as if someone were next to her in the bed. Suddenly, the sheets fell and the bed shifted again as if someone had just gotten out of it. But there was no one there! Would you stay in a bed you might have to share with a ghost? Well, the mother and daughter didn't! They packed up their things and asked to move to a different room.

CHAPTER 4

Victoria's Black Swan Inn

Only a few short miles from the city center and the Alamo sits a former dairy plantation, nestled along a dirt track. It is along this dusty road, which runs between two major thoroughfares in the heart of San Antonio, you will find Victoria's Black Swan Inn, a beautiful pre–American Civil War structure that includes the main house, a dairy barn, and many other outbuildings on the banks of Salado Creek.

These days, the house and grounds provide a pastoral setting in the middle of the city for weddings and ghost tours.

Yes, ghost tours! That's because the inn is said to be home to nearly a dozen different spirits. Some of the spirits might be from one of the pivotal battles in the fight for Texas's independence from Mexico. Or they could be a farmer, his sons, or even children who lived here over 150 years ago. Whoever, or whatever, these spirits are, they make Victoria's Black Swan Inn one of the most haunted places in all of Texas.

Long before any of the current structures on the property were built, the area was home to Native Americans. Even though there were numerous indigenous populations, Spanish explorers in the early 1500s collectively called the groups Coahuiltecans (pronounced *kwa-weel-ta-kahns*), a name that refers to the area in which the Spanish encountered the indigenous peoples. At the time, the Mexican state of Coahuila ran along a segment of the Rio Grande, reaching several hundred miles south into present-day Mexico and north into what became San Antonio. Beginning in the late 1600s, other indigenous groups such as the Lipan Apache, the Tonkawa, and the Comanche migrated to the area after being forced out of their lands farther north.

Archaeological artifacts on the Black Swan property provide evidence of dwellings and a sweat lodge used for ceremonies, while researchers believe a burial ground lies under the main house. Maybe the burial ground gave rise to a spirit roaming through the home's halls. How would you feel if your home were built on top of a cemetery?

Fishing along the creek was likely a major source of food for the Native Americans, and people still like to reel in bluegill or carp. Occasionally, anglers enjoying quality time luring dinner have been chased off by what appear to be the ghosts of Native American children. Others have heard faint drum beats and seen wisps of smoke rising in the air as if the sweat lodge is still hosting important tribal gatherings hundreds of years later. Maybe these rituals were so important that even death cannot stop them.

Six and a half years after the fall of the Alamo, the banks of Salado Creek were witness to a pivotal battle between Texian soldiers and the Mexican Army on September 17, 1842. Mexican general Adrian Woll led his troops to battle in an attempt to retake the Texas territory, which had declared its independence from Mexico in 1836. That declaration did not end hostilities, and a years-long struggle to retain independence followed. The Battle of Salado Creek was the decisive victory the Texas Rangers needed to end hostilities with Mexico for good.

Colonel Matthew Caldwell knew his regiment of Texas Rangers was outnumbered, with only 200 militia members to fight against 1,600 Mexican soldiers, so he sent out requests for reinforcements. Even though he only had one-eighth the number of soldiers,

Caldwell defeated the Mexican Army. General Woll and his army retreated that night and returned to Mexico after losing sixty men on the battlefield. The Texians lost only one man, Stephen Jett, who was trying to save his horse.

Caldwell's request for reinforcements was heard, though not many soldiers made it to Salado Creek before the battle was over. The Mexican Army overtook Captain Nicholas Dawson and fifty-three soldiers less than one mile from the Battle of Salado Creek and on the north end of the current Black Swan Inn property. Thirty-six of Dawson's unit were killed, two escaped, and fifteen were taken prisoner. Only nine prisoners survived. Caldwell learned of Dawson's defeat the next day.

Ever since both battles ended, visions of Texian and Mexican soldiers have been reported, almost as if spirits are reenacting the battle, like on a video loop. A lone soldier is often spotted near the gazebo on the property. Some people think he might be Jett, the only Texian fatality that day, searching for his horse. The bugle that Black Swan guests hear echoing in the air might be a battle call to the soldiers or a tribute to their many fallen comrades.

Twenty-five years after Texas's independence was finally settled by the Battle of Salado Creek, Sebastien Rippstein and his wife settled on the property and built a milking house and a stone house barn, which was just what it sounds like: a house with a connected barn. It was a common style of building in Europe, where the Rippsteins were from. House barns provided heat to the living areas from the body heat of the animals. They were also a way to protect the animals from thieves or predators, and farmers do not need to walk outside in inclement weather to feed their livestock.

The Mahlers, Henry and Marie, purchased the property in 1887, and several generations of the family lived on and expanded the property and buildings until it was sold to the Holbrook and Woods families in 1941. The Holbrooks expanded the main mansion and purchased more property.

In 1952, Hall Park Street and his wife, Jolene, inherited the house from her mother. They lived there until they died in 1965 and 1959, respectively. Hall died under mysterious circumstances. The official cause of death was suicide. Local legend says his death was staged to resemble suicide, but it is suspected he was murdered because of a secret treasure he kept in the house. If he was hiding something, it has never been found. Perhaps the treasure was real and it was stolen. We may never know the answer to the puzzle.

Did you know the collective noun for a group of ghosts is "congress," "knight," or "press"? A congress certainly does appear to roam the buildings of Victoria's Black Swan Inn. It's no wonder when you consider the ancient burial sites, the two violent battles fought on the property, and the many former residents who died here.

Many visitors to the inn have witnessed strange apparitions in nearly every part of the property. The milking house and dairy are host to several phenomena, including visions of a man in an undershirt watching people through barn windows, occasionally shouting "Get out!" at them.

Maybe it is Henry Mahler, who was proud of his dairy and continues looking after his herd. He is occasionally seen at the main house as well outside an upstairs windows at night, staring malevolently at guests. Whoever it may be has scared away guests, and that room is rarely requested.

Another male spirit roams the halls of the main house, especially in the south wing. It seems Hall Park Street searches for his beloved

Jolene, who died six years before he did. Or maybe he guards the treasure many insisted was his downfall.

A woman in white frequents the main house as well. She wears a beautiful gown, a beaded headband, and a feather adornment in her hair. Witnesses say she walks out of the main house, floats across a small knoll, and stops at a gazebo, where she seems to ponder something before disappearing. Jolene may be dressed for one of the lavish parties she was famous for. Or maybe she came across the spirit of Stephen Jett when she was alive and wonders if he still drifts amid the gardens.

Guests mention seeing a young girl playing tricks on unsuspecting visitors or jumping on mattresses. Henry Mahler's daughter Sara might be the trickster. Or it is more likely to be Henry's granddaughter Sophia who lived in the house as an unmarried woman until she died in her eighties, although she loved a good prank as a young girl.

Because Victoria's Black Swan Inn has so much activity, the current owner allowed television crews to film throughout the property. As a result, the inn appeared on TV several times with paranormal experts attempting to figure out which spirits may be behind all the experiences people have had here.

One expert says three entities haunt the barn, and all of them seem aggressive toward women. She suggests these entities are likely Henry Mahler, Sebastien Rippstein, and his son Gustav. Another expert believes a woman often seen sitting on the edge of a bed in one particular room is Jolene Street's grandmother, who spent several years in ill health, confined to the room she now never leaves.

During one filming session, the spirits of children harassed crew members. One presence bit a crew member on the leg, and another pinched the crew. They also moved filming equipment and scattered it about the woods of the property.

Perhaps the most compelling experience was when the experts attempted to contact a spirit in the main house. They began recording one expert as he asked a series of questions.

No response.

But then he asked, "Do you know the names of the children who live in this house?" A woman's voice answered clearly. When the expert played the recording for the owner, she said it sounded like her mother, who had recently died in the home. Later, another recording captured the same voice using a specific "code word" the owner and her mother had agreed on so the mother could come back after her death and confirm she was okay. The owner explained she had never shared the code word with anyone, and only her mother could have known it.

If you would like to see for yourself whether Texian soldiers, Gustav Rippstein, Henry Mahler, or any of the other former residents still wander the banks of Salado Creek, you are welcome to visit Victoria's Black Swan Inn and join one of the monthly ghost tours. Or you can sign up to be an actual ghost hunter at one of their regular paranormal investigations on the property. Maybe you can find Hall Park Street's treasure—with his help, of course.

The Menger Hotel

CHAPTER 5

The Menger Hotel

Trauma tends to leave a psychic wound, according to paranormal researchers. It's no wonder the Menger Hotel—located right across the road from the Alamo and within the area of the battlefield—is considered one of the most haunted spots in all of San Antonio.

Built in 1859 by William Menger and his wife, Mary, the hotel began as a boardinghouse before being converted into a luxury hotel steps away from the famous fort. Menger also built the city's first brewery, introducing beer to San Antonio. The success of the brewery led to an increase in tourism, which in turn led to the need for something more than the boardinghouse.

The new hotel saw famous guests such as General Robert E. Lee, General Ulysses S. Grant, and Theodore Roosevelt. At the time, Roosevelt was a lieutenant colonel during the Spanish-American War. In 1898, he used the bar of the Menger Hotel to recruit his famous Rough Riders, also known as the 1st US Volunteer Cavalry.

The US Army needed more soldiers to help in the fight against the Spanish Army in Cuba. Roosevelt used his popularity to recruit volunteers. Legend has it he rode his horse into the bar to draw attention to the volunteer

opportunity. The table at which he sat to sign volunteers is still in the bar today.

Both General Grant and Theodore Roosevelt went on to become US presidents, and the hotel later hosted other presidents, including William McKinley, William Taft, Woodrow Wilson, Harry Truman, Lyndon Johnson, Richard Nixon, Ronald Reagan, George H.W. Bush, and Bill Clinton.

Despite these famous people spending time here, it was not all fun times at the hotel. In the early days, there were no nearby hospitals, and people who lived on the outskirts of San Antonio or in nearby smaller towns had limited access to doctors. One solution for someone who was sick or for a woman ready to give birth was to travel to the Menger Hotel, rent a room, and summon a doctor from town. Being closer to the doctor made it more likely someone would survive. Of course, not everyone did.

Staff and guests of the hotel say some of those ghosts still roam the halls of the Menger Hotel.

One of the more famous resident ghosts is Captain Richard King, who ran a steamboat company that provided blockade runners on the Mississippi River during the Civil War. Blockade runners were specially built steamboats the Confederate Army used to push their way through the Union Navy's strategic blockade along the Gulf of Mexico, the Atlantic Ocean, and up into the Mississippi River. The Union blockade tried to prevent Confederate forces from trading for supplies like weapons, food, tobacco, and more. Often, the blockade runners carried cotton to trade with the Bahamas, Cuba, and as far away as England for supplies they could not find on Confederate soil. Many of the owners of blockade runners became wealthy as a result of the trading. Captain King was no exception.

After the war, King traveled to Corpus Christi, Texas, and founded a cattle ranch. His King Ranch was so successful he added to his wealth to become one of the richest cattle barons in Texas. The ranch remains open to visitors today, allowing a glimpse into Texas history. King frequently traveled to San Antonio on ranch business, and he stayed at the Menger Hotel so often he had his own private suite.

It was in this suite King died of stomach cancer in 1885. The lobby of the hotel hosted

his funeral, and thousands of King's friends and acquaintances attended. But the funeral was not the last anyone saw of Captain King.

The King Suite still contains a few pieces of the captain's furniture, including the bed in which he died. Some people brave enough to sleep there say they have seen him standing above the bed staring down at them. Others have heard him walking around the room, opening and closing shutters. He occasionally roams other areas of the hotel, seeming to pass through the door to his suite to wander down hallways before retracing his steps and disappearing once more into his suite.

An unusual red orb floats above a chair and his bed yet appears nowhere else in the hotel. If you are brave enough, you could spend the night in the King Suite of the Menger Hotel and find out for yourself if this orb is King's ghostly energy still pulsing through his old rooms.

While Theodore Roosevelt did not die at the hotel, he must have had a special attachment to the place, because he still appears to people on occasion. Those who have seen him say he calls out to bar patrons, seeking more volunteers for the Rough Riders.

One employee at the bar says when he was still new to the job, he was closing up for the night when he heard a noise behind him. Knowing there was no one else in the room, the frightened employee slowly turned around to find Teddy Roosevelt standing at the bar, staring him down. More frightened than curious, the employee ran to the doors to escape, but they were locked. He banged on them, calling for help. Once help arrived and the young man explained what happened, Roosevelt's ghost was gone. It's possible Teddy was still looking for volunteers. If so, he

might have disappeared when he realized the employee wasn't brave enough to make a very good Rough Rider.

But not all the ghosts in the Menger Hotel were rich or famous. Sallie White loved her job as a hotel chambermaid. Her employers loved her, too. Unfortunately for Sallie, her husband was not as beloved. He was abusive and frequently violent with Sallie.

One night, after a particularly nasty fight, Sallie ran out of her house two streets away from the hotel, trying to escape her husband's rage. He followed her and pulled a gun, shooting her in the back. Sallie didn't die right away but was brought to the hotel, where she lingered in agony for two days before finally slipping away. Because Sallie was such a beloved employee, the hotel covered her funeral costs. The hotel framed the receipt as a reminder of their cherished chambermaid.

Sallie still tends to her duties at the hotel, carrying towels in and out of guest rooms or dusting furniture in the hallways, all while still dressed in her uniform. One guest, while watching TV, saw Sallie walk through the closed door into the room. She held clean towels and walked straight for the restroom, walking through yet another closed door.

Another guest climbed out of the shower and went back into the room to dress. There was Sallie, standing at the end of the bed folding laundry. The woman said she could see right through the chambermaid. But she was there all the same.

This could be Sallie's way of saying thank you to her former employers for their kindness to her, even in death. Everyone appreciates being appreciated, don't you think?

Among many other ghosts, guests of the hotel have reported seeing a Spanish conquistador in full armor or the spirits of ranchers who stopped at the hotel during cattle drives. But the story of a nameless young girl may be the saddest yet.

In the late 1800s, a young girl was tragically run over by a horse and carriage right outside the hotel. The girl's name and exact age are lost to history, but hotel employees nicknamed her Sarah. Like Sallie, Sarah is a sweet ghost, despite the circumstances of her death. The staff of the hotel say Sarah likes to play pranks. She occasionally calls out employees' names late at night as they clean the Colonial Restaurant in the hotel. But when employees turn around, Sarah is not there, as if she is playing hide-and-seek with someone.

Once, Sarah ran by an employee and grabbed her by the waist, maybe trying to tickle the employee. Sometimes, she charges up to the front desk, tossing papers and brochures in the air, laughing as she goes. One employee took a photo inside the hotel, and who should appear in the background but a young girl with long dark hair and a white dress. Maybe this is Sarah, trying to make sure she is not forgotten.

Now that you know more about the Menger Hotel and its ghostly guests, it's time to make your reservation, check out the King Suite, and look for Sallie as she tidies your room. If you see Teddy Roosevelt, will you volunteer to join his Rough Riders?

Texas Chisholm Trail

CHAPTER 6

The Sporting District

Many years after the Battle of Salado Creek, after Texas was annexed by the United States and became a state in 1845, the expansion of the railroads brought a rise in tourism in San Antonio. Patriotic Texans wanted to "remember the Alamo" and see where James Bowie, Davy Crockett, and so many others gave up their lives to defend their country.

After the Civil War, San Antonio's location along the Chisolm Trail also brought ranchers, herders, and cattlemen to the city as they drove cattle from southern Texas north into Kansas to sell. Men on horseback who led the cattle along the trail were known as drovers, and they made the arduous, nearly one-thousand-mile journey, sometimes with hundreds of cattle. But why would drovers make such a difficult trip in the first place?

During the American Civil War, Texas farmers were not allowed to sell their cattle to other states. After the war, Texas had too many cattle, but states in the north didn't have many at all. As a result, prices for cattle were as low as four dollars a head in Texas and closer to ten times that amount in Kansas. Cattlemen all over Texas not only made the journey, but they made a lot of money as well. Historians estimate over five million cattle traveled north on the Chisolm Trail until railroads figured out how to transport the animals with more efficiency.

All those tourists and drovers brought lots of money to San Antonio, and they wanted to spend it. The city was more than happy to oblige. In an approximately ten-square-block area, numerous businesses provided diversions such as live theater, saloons, gambling, dance halls, and more. At the time, these establishments were either illegal or frowned upon, which is why they were confined to what city officials called the Sporting District.

For twenty-five cents, travelers could purchase the local guidebook, which listed the different businesses in the district. Called *The Blue Book*, its subtitle, "For Visitors, Tourists and Those Seeking a Good Time while in San Antonio, Texas," was a polite way of saying, "For Those Seeking Illicit Amusement."

Historians say Billy Kleiman, a former Rough Rider with Teddy Roosevelt and former police officer, published *The Blue Book* to boost patronage for his business, the Beauty Saloon. It worked. Billy became the wealthiest man in San Antonio. At least he was, until he was killed in a shooting incident at another saloon.

Shootings like the one that killed Kleiman were common in the Sporting District. But they were by no means the only peril for customers or employees of the many businesses in the area. Nellie Clemente, a saloon girl and an actress in the Washington Variety Theater, was jilted by one of the many patrons of the local saloons. She was said to be so distraught over the loss that she died by suicide. Whether she was in Kleiman's saloon, the theater, or some other location is not clear. But with so many "women in white" reported in various locations throughout the Sporting District, Nellie could very well still be mourning her broken heart.

The woman in white sometimes appears at Casa Navarro, a homestead originally built by Texas patriot José Antonio Navarro, who lived there from 1832 until his death in 1871. Soon after his death, the house became

a popular saloon and drinking den in the Sporting District. By the 1960s, the home had been reclaimed by city officials and became a historical museum documenting the Navarro family's patriotism and contributions to the Texas Revolution.

The building still stands today, and employees tell tales of a woman roaming the property after all the visitors are gone and lights are off. Wearing white, she wanders the property as if she were lost. Sometimes, she stops to peer out the windows, where passersby have noticed her staring. They've also noticed lights turning off and on at night, but when asked about it, employees have confirmed no one was on the property at these times. Maybe this sad-looking woman is the ghost of Nellie Clemente, or she might be the ghost of an employee of

a former saloon on the property, murdered by a jealous customer, and now her spirit roams the property at night. Whoever she is and whatever she is searching for, she will forever search in vain.

The woman in white isn't seen only at Casa Navarro. She appears at another popular establishment known as Fannie Porter's Sporting House. In the early 1900s, Fannie was well liked by tourists because she valued discretion and never divulged her customers' identities to local authorities. The Wild Bunch, a gang of outlaws led by Butch Cassidy and his right-hand man, Harry Longabaugh (also known as the Sundance Kid), frequently stayed at Fannie Porter's Sporting House. But she never turned in any of the felons.

One account says during one of his visits to San Antonio, Cassidy rode a bicycle up and down the street in front of the Sporting House hoping to impress Fannie and her employees. Bikes were a novelty back then, so Fannie might have been captivated indeed. In 1969, actor Paul Newman played the role of Butch in a movie called *Butch Cassidy and the Sundance Kid*, and he recreated the famous bicycle story on screen.

While the building is now in private hands, ghost stories still abound. When the building

was a center for families in crisis, people often felt cold spots or heard soft singing as they walked the hallways. Fannie is said to bustle about, looking after her employees and guarding her patrons' secrets. Another woman in white paces in the front of the building and often waves at passersby. When people take photos of the building, orbs of light or a cloudy outline of a woman in the picture frequently appear in the photo. Whether the woman is Nellie wandering from building to building throughout the district in search of her lost love or Fannie greeting her customers and continuing business as usual, it's clear someone's spirit remains connected to the Sporting District, choosing to stay close to strong memories.

As San Antonio continued to grow, it became a strong military city. In 1941, just a few months before the United States was attacked at Pearl Harbor and joined World War II, General Dwight D. Eisenhower decided the Sporting District was not an appropriate place for young men representing our country to

spend their time. He worked with San Antonio city officials, and the entertainment district was shut down for good. Many years later, in 1953, Eisenhower became the thirty-fourth president of the United States.

Although Eisenhower shut down the district, he did not shut down the spirits of those who lived, worked, let loose, or died there. They still have stories to tell if you listen carefully.

The Bexar County Courthouse

CHAPTER 7

Old Bexar County Jail

It's not unusual for a building to be constructed for one purpose only to have it change years later. Hotel Gibbs began life as an office building. The Emily Morgan Hotel began as a medical complex before becoming offices. But it is unusual for a jail to be turned into a hotel.

If you visited San Antonio years ago and checked in to the hotel on the corner of Commerce and Camaron Streets, you would have been sleeping in the Old Bexar (pronounced *bay-har)* County Jail. It's fitting the jail became a hotel—the jail was once nicknamed "the Shrimp Hotel" because of its location on Camaron, which is Spanish for "shrimp."

Built in 1878, the two-story jail was expanded in 1911 when a third story was added. But it wasn't the only change made. In the early days of the jail, prisoners were often executed in public, usually outside on temporary gallows. The entire town attended, including children, who were given the day off from school for the event. Public hangings were meant to be a deterrent, to show what happened to criminals if they were caught breaking the law. But during the 1911 expansion, the architect designed an indoor gallows away from the public eye. No longer would children witness such a gruesome event.

The jail expanded again in 1928, when two additional stories were added. The jail now stood at five stories tall. Eventually, the jail closed down in 1962 when it became

overcrowded and there was no space left to expand. A new jail was built in another location. For years, the building sat as an archival storage facility for the city until it was purchased in 2002 and turned into a hotel. Because the jail was considered a historic building, city regulations required the new owners to leave the bars on all the windows, so you might have had to sleep in a hotel room that felt like a prison cell!

As you might expect, prisons housed not only criminals but all manner of sad tales that made for good ghost stories. Hotel guests have often seen, heard, and felt things in the rooms and halls of the hotel. Many guests complained of cold spots in their rooms, even in the height of the scorching San Antonio summers. Oddly, turning off the air-conditioning and turning on the heat didn't help. The cold spots remained. Paranormal experts think ghosts need energy to appear. They might make lights flicker when they pull from electricity in a room. Sometimes, they pull energy directly from the air, which would explain cold spots that seemed to linger, despite the Texas heat.

Numerous signs throughout the hotel requested guests leave the windows closed because of their age. Yet guests returned to their rooms to find windows open and lights on. Occasionally, guests contacted the front desk to complain of whispers during the night. Some said men's voices singing in their ears woke them. In the breakfast room, the staff of the hotel frequently had to rearrange furniture and dishes moved during the night. Spirits didn't pay attention to signs, locked doors, or quiet hours. They simply did what they wanted, when they wanted.

The most unsettling encounter came from a mother and son who spent the day sightseeing in San Antonio. When they returned to their room, the mother noticed the housekeeping

staff had cleaned the whole room but had forgotten to make the bed. She noticed an indentation in the bedding as if a person were lying there. As she reached out to straighten the covers, the indentation vanished. She placed her hand on the spot, and it was still warm! The mother and son immediately asked for a new room.

In 2020, the old Bexar County Jail was demolished to make way for new construction. Whatever was behind all these ghostly events will forever remain a mystery—unless you go to the new building and discover eerie cold spots, disembodied voices, or furniture moved in the night!

Historic Tower in Comanche Lookout Park

CHAPTER 8

Comanche Lookout Hill

On the outskirts of San Antonio, about twenty miles northwest of the Alamo, an unusual structure towers over old Native American hunting grounds. It sits atop Comanche Lookout Hill and resembles the ruins of an old castle.

Legend says the local Apache and Comanche people used the top of the hill as a lookout when hunting, giving the area its name. The nearby Cibolo Creek provided water for animals, making Comanche Lookout the perfect spot for hunters to watch from the safety of the hill and plan the best way to approach any game.

Studies of the area performed by the Center for Archaeological Research at the University of Texas–San Antonio have found remnants of prehistoric tools, campsites, and a chert quarry in the area. Chert, also known as flint, is a sedimentary rock Native Americans used to make tools because the stone was easy to split, or knap, to make sharp edges for arrowheads, knife blades, and hand axes.

With access to water, good hunting, and a plentiful supply of raw material for weapons and tools, Comanche Lookout Hill became a valuable resource to other groups who frequently battled with the Native Americans for control of the area. Many battles make for many ghosts.

Control and ownership of the hill went through numerous hands until retired US Army colonel Edward Coppock acquired the land in the early twentieth century. After forty-four years with the Army, during which he traveled the world, Coppock had grand plans to erect a castle resembling the one built by William the Conqueror of England on the site of the Battle of Hastings in the eleventh century. The castle plans included stone towers on all corners of a U-shaped foundation.

By 1948, Coppock and his sons managed to build one of the four-story corner towers, a stone lodge, several outbuildings, a water tower, a corral, a barbecue pit, tennis courts, and some smaller homes. Sadly, Coppock would not live to build the rest of his dream castle. After his death that year, a fire ravaged everything but the Norman-style tower. His sons abandoned their father's project and sold the land in 1968.

For three more decades, the land sat idle until the City of San Antonio purchased it and turned it into a park. The tower still stands on top of the hill, where people have seen and heard strange things.

Some visitors say that as they walk up the hill, rhythmic drumbeats become louder and louder the closer they are to the tower. Upon reaching the top, the drumbeats sometimes turn into hammering noises. Others hear chanting, though they can't make out the words. The drumbeats and chanting could be lingering sounds of ancient Apache and Comanche hunting rituals, while the hammering could be echoes of flint knapping or tower construction.

Whenever rumors of haunted buildings abound, there will be ghosthunters attempting to make contact. Colonel Coppock must not approve of such shenanigans, because he has often been spotted in the tower glowering down on the ghosthunters with a stern glint in his eye. Other ghosthunters have watched as the colonel pushes a stone-filled wheelbarrow around the hill, trying in death to build the dream castle he failed to erect in life.

Some hikers claim to be followed by dark outlines of people wearing a camouflage of sticks and leaves in their hair. These "shadowmen" chase anyone on the trail, especially after sundown. It's possible the ancient indigenous residents

still guard the hill that was so important to their lifestyle.

One evening, a woman was walking up Comanche Lookout Hill with her dog. She often heard chanting or yelling coming from the woods as she walked, but she always thought it was kids. On this particular walk, however, her dog turned to look behind them, growling, and the fur on his back rose. When the woman turned around to see why her dog was upset, she saw what appeared to be two men who suddenly let out a bellow and charged toward her and the dog. Without waiting to see what they wanted, she raced down the hill as fast as she and the dog could run, only stopping when she reached the parking lot. To her surprise, the park had closed, and hers was the only car left. She had been alone on the hill all along.

If you're brave enough, you could wander the woods in search of the drumbeats, stand up to fierce men chasing you down the trail, or hike to the peak of Comanche Lookout Hill and search for Colonel Coppock. While you're there, you can offer to push his wheelbarrow, if you dare!

CHAPTER 9

The Huebner-Onion House

On the northwest side of San Antonio, in the small suburb of Leon Valley, sits the old homestead of Joseph Huebner, an Austrian immigrant who settled in the area in 1858 and built his home in 1862. Huebner (pronounced *heeb-ner*) later turned his home into a stagecoach stop, because there was nowhere for travelers to rest or feed the horses on the trail from Bandera to San Antonio.

In those days, a stagecoach with one team of four horses could travel about four to five miles per hour, depending on terrain, weather, and weight of the coach and cargo. So the nearly sixty-mile trip from Bandera to San Antonio would typically take a minimum of twelve hours. That's assuming all conditions were perfect. However, it left no time to stop for passengers and horses to eat or for the team to rest.

In practical terms, stagecoaches averaged about twenty-five to thirty miles per day once rest breaks for the horses were factored in. Even though passengers sat in the coach the whole way, it was uncomfortable to be jostled about in a contraption with wooden or wood-and-metal wheels and no shock absorbers. Unlike modern cars, the seats in a stagecoach might not have had cushions or upholstery. So every bump, rut, or rock on the path could be felt on passengers' backsides, making frequent rest breaks a necessity.

For a trip from Bandera to San Antonio, what would take us a little over an hour in our cars took stagecoach travelers about two days. As the only stop on the route, Joseph Huebner's home became an important feature of the stagecoach trail, and he became a wealthy man as a result.

Rich as he was, he may not have been a particularly smart man. One night in 1882, after a wagon hauling liquor stopped for the night, Huebner bought a bottle of whiskey from the driver. After finishing the bottle, he went to the wagon, grabbed a second bottle, and took a huge swig. What Huebner didn't realize was the cargo also contained kerosene. After downing a mouthful of kerosene, Huebner stumbled back into his house,

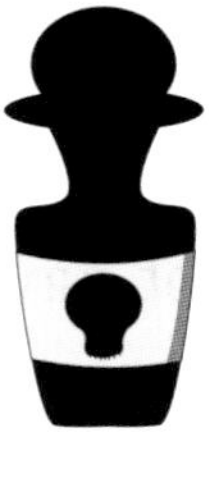

where he collapsed and died. The family buried their patriarch on the property a stone's throw from the main house. Shortly after his death, the hauntings began.

A new family moved into the home in the early 1930s. Judge John Onion Sr. and his wife, Harriet, a schoolteacher, had fallen in love with the charm and character of the old stagecoach stop and made it their family home. Shortly after moving in, the family experienced what they believed was Joseph Huebner wandering about the property.

The Onions heard footsteps throughout the house, including on the stairs. John Onion Jr. wrote about the eerie echoes of boots on wood, saying to him it sounded as if someone were trying to tiptoe up the stairs and avoid the creaky spots, which made uneven footsteps, with some loud, some quiet, sometimes one right after the other and sometimes with long periods in between. He wrote, "When I was . . . in bed, I had my eyes glued to the door to see who might walk in." But he wasn't expecting someone in his family. He was sure it was a ghost!

Because the family was upper-middle class, they owned some of the finer conveniences of modern living. This included an iron. It wasn't what we think of today, a small appliance plugging into the wall and gliding over clothes to smooth them out. Instead, the Onions had a large machine iron, similar to what modern dry cleaners or industrial laundries might use. A machine iron came in a box about two feet square. When the lid of the box was removed, the sides and front of the box folded down to make a kind of table. In the center of the box was the iron, which sat over a heating element and motor. The back piece of the iron was a roller arm wrapped in soft cotton batting and covered with flannel. In front of the roller arm was a "shoe," or a curved, smooth-surface metal plate that conformed to the roller arm.

To use the iron, a heating element needed to be switched on, and then fabric was inserted between the arm and the shoe. When a knee pedal was pressed, the shoe lifted into place against the roller arm, which then rotated, pulling fabric between the shoe and arm, smoothing out the wrinkles. When the knee pedal was released, wrinkle-free fabric emerged. As you might expect, the motor made a lot of noise, as did the roller arm and shoe clamping together and releasing.

One summer morning, when John Jr. was about thirteen or fourteen, he was asleep on a second-story screened-in porch because the house had no air-conditioning, and it had been unbearable inside the night before. When his father left for work, the tires on the gravel

woke John, who lay there for a few minutes rubbing the sleep from his eyes. He heard his mother in the room down the hall and listened to the familiar click of the knee pedal, the thunk of the arm and shoe connecting, the drone of the motor, the click of the pedal, the releasing knock of arm and shoe. This pattern continued for a few more minutes, and then John decided to head down to breakfast. As he passed the room, the machine continued. When he arrived in the kitchen, there was his mother! She asked John if he'd been fiddling with her iron, and John said, "No, I thought you were." She told him she had been in the kitchen preparing breakfast since before his father had left for work. They both went upstairs to look in the room where the machine sat, quiet, still, and cold to the touch. John said he would never be able to explain it.

In a recorded interview, Harriet Onion spoke of unexplained incidents over the years. Very often, the family would all be together and hear the footsteps her son wrote about, sometimes on the stairs, sometimes in hallways, and occasionally outside. A piano on the first floor played when no one was in the room. She felt certain it was the spirits of the Huebner family. She'd heard rumors about Joseph Huebner's death, and neighbors said he might not have died from kerosene poisoning and may have been buried alive. Joseph Huebner could still be trying to get someone's attention to this very day!

After the last Onion family member passed away in the home in 1983, the homestead sat empty for quite some time and became a common hangout for thrill-seeking kids hoping for a glimpse of Joseph. They told tales of hearing wagon wheels crunching over the gravel, the clop of horses' hooves trotting up to the main house, or soft piano music lingering in the air.

These days, the Huebner-Onion House is an important landmark preserved by the Leon Valley Historical Society. It is not open to the public, but maybe you can drive by and see if Joseph Huebner still wanders the property trying to let people know he is still "alive."

San Antonio is filled with history, some of it violent and some of it sad. But fiercely independent Texians wanted more than to be a

Mexican territory, and that independent streak led to the battles that earned independence from Mexico and paved the way for the territory to become its own country. This big thinking is still at the heart of Texas culture. And as the saying goes, "Everything is bigger in Texas." Even the ghost stories!

Jay Whistler was born on Halloween and grew up in a haunted house. She loves listening to ghost stories, whether real or imagined, and willingly explores haunted places on her travels across the country and around the globe. Even so, she will always be afraid of the dark. The boring part is that Jay has her MFA in Writing from Vermont College of Fine Arts.

Check out some of the other Spooky America titles available now!

Spooky America was adapted from the creeptastic Haunted America series for adults. Haunted America explores historical haunts in cities and regions across America. Each book chronicles both the widely known and less-familiar history behind local ghosts and other unexplained mysteries. Here's more from *Haunted History of Old San Antonio* authors Lauren M. Swartz and James A. Swartz:

For more, visit SistersGrimmGhostTours.com.